# BRITANNICA DISCOVERY LIBRARY

**7**

# SHAPES

*In this book, you will:*

**discover** interesting things about shapes.

**learn** new words.

**answer** fun questions.

**play** a shape matching game.

**find** more shape activities at the back of the book.

ENCYCLOPÆDIA
## Britannica®

CHICAGO   LONDON   NEW DELHI   PARIS   SEOUL   SYDNEY   TAIPEI   TOKYO

Deep in the earth lies a tiny seed.
The shape of this seed is round.

The seed will burst open and become
something new
as it grows beneath the ground.

Slowly a plant takes shape from the seed
as it's warmed by the sun and watered by rain.

Just as the plant changes shape as it grows,
your shape will change too, again and again!

Think of cars and boats, animals and toys.
All of these things have got their own shapes.
We can recognise many things
in our world by their shapes.

How many of the shapes on these pages can you name?

# Some things can be many different shapes

There are so many cars on the road,
but the cars don't all look the same.
They are different shapes. But they are all still cars.

Look at the boats and bicycles moving by.
They are all different shapes too!

# Houses also have got many different shapes

Your house may look a lot like the other houses in your neighbourhood.

Do any of these houses look like yours?

But it might have a very different shape than houses in other parts of the world.

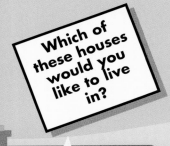

Which of these houses would you like to live in?

Tell a story about people living in one of these houses.

9

Look closely at the different trees shown here. They are all different shapes. But the leaves on each tree have got the same shape.

Can you match the big leaves shown here with the tree that they belong to?

11

Some things stay the same shape unless something happens to change them.

Ice cubes melt when the air is warm.
Clouds change shape before a storm.

Blow up a balloon and just like that,
you've got a balloon that's big and fat!

Bubble gum gets soft and gooey
as soon as you start to chew it.

Many shapes have got special names.

These names help us to talk
about the world around us.

On some nights, the moon
looks as round as a ball.
Other times it looks curved.

The windows in your house
may all be square.
The front door is probably a rectangle.

Look around
the room you
are in. How
many shapes
can you
name?

Some shapes are called open shapes.
Others are closed shapes.

A curve is a kind of open shape.
All the shapes on this page are
open shapes.

Closed shapes haven't got openings.
If you draw a closed shape, the line
will end up right where it began.
All the shapes on this page
are closed shapes.

Look around the room you are in. Find three closed shapes. See if you can find three open shapes.

17

A circle is always round and flat.
Wheels are shaped like circles.
Most plates are circles too.

Can you name the things in this picture that are circles?

Can you name the things in this picture that are spheres?

ome things have got a round shape, but they are not flat.
This kind of shape is called a **sphere.**
Basketballs and tennis balls and snowballs
re all shaped like spheres.

19

A rectangle is a flat shape with four sides and four L-shaped corners. Flags are often rectangles. So are many windows. The blanket on your bed is probably a rectangle too.

Can you name the things in this picture that are rectangles?

Some rectangles have got four sides that are all the same length. We call this special kind of rectangle a square.

Picture frames and postage stamps are often square-shaped.

Can you name the things in this picture that are square?

Most boxes have got a top, a bottom, and four sides. Altogether this makes six sides.

Sometimes all six of these sides are square. Then we call the shape a **cube.**

Can you find the cubes on these pages?

22

The **triangle** is a flat shape with three corners and three sides.

Sometimes triangles have got three equal sides. Other triangles have got sides of different lengths.

Can you find the triangles on these pages?

Some buildings have got a square bottom and sides shaped like triangles.
The sides meet at a point at the top.
This kind of shape is called a **pyramid.**

Long ago, huge pyramids were built in Egypt. Today some cities have got buildings shaped like pyramids too.

Can you find the pyramids on these pages?

Triangle. Rectangle. Pyramid. Square.
Circle, cube, and sphere.
How many of these shapes can *you* find
in the picture here?

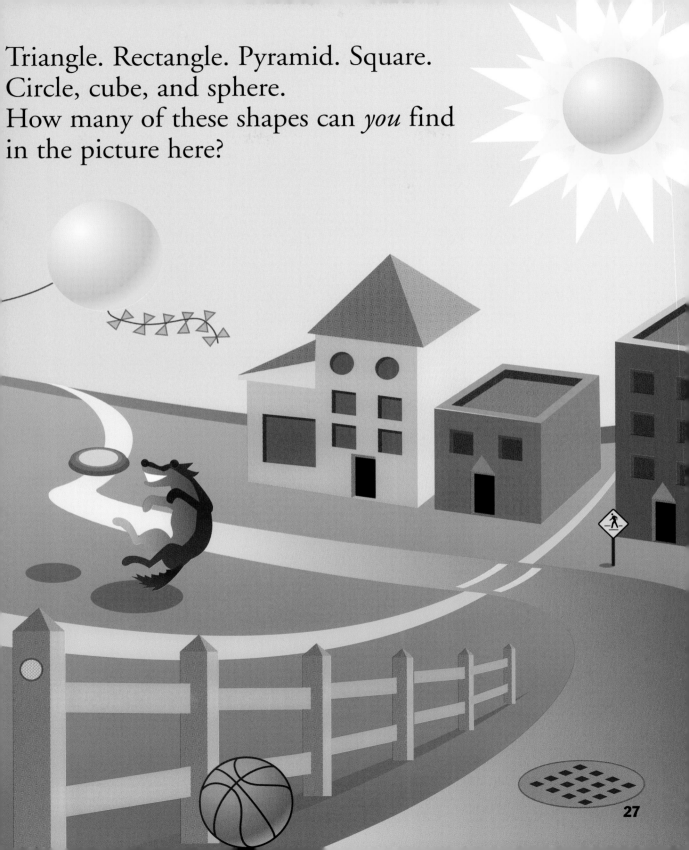

Our eyes see the shapes of things.
Our brains help us tell the difference
between these shapes.

We know a closed shape and an open shape.
We can tell if something is a square, a circle,
a cube, or a sphere. We see the difference
between a rectangle and
a triangle.

All the different shapes that we see mak

the world a very interesting place!

CAVAN COUNTY
LIBRARY

29

# SHAPES
## GLOSSARY

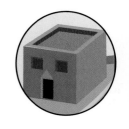

**cube** (kyoob)  a shape with six square sides all of the same size

**pyramid** (PEER ah mid) a shape with a flat base and three or more sides shaped like triangles that meet in a point at the top

**sphere** (sfeer)  a round shape in which every part of the outside is as close to the centre as every other part

**triangle** (TRY ang uhl)  a flat, closed shape with three sides and three corners

# Fun Ways to Learn About SHAPES

## Where Is My Shape?

**1** How many circle, square, triangle, and rectangle shapes can you and your friends spy in a single room?

Take it in turns and try this: The first person chooses something in the room but does not say what it is. Give clues only. Say, for example, 'I spy a triangle.' Let the others try to guess what you've picked. If no one guesses it right away, add hints that describe the thing you have picked, like, 'I spy a red triangle' or 'I spy a striped circle.'

Once someone guesses your shape correctly, take turns until everyone has had a chance to describe a shape in the room.

## Shapes Treasure Hunt

**2** With a friend, see how many of the same shapes you can find around the house. Each person playing should look just for one or two shapes. Maybe one person will look for squares and triangles. Another one will look only for circles and pyramids (hard to find!). Someone else might hunt for rectangles and spheres.

Only one thing of each kind will count - you can only collect one penny, for example, not ten! Set a time limit, such as 15 minutes. The person who can collect the most correct shapes in that time is the winner!

## Shapes in the Bag

**3** Play this game with one other person. Each person collects five or ten small, differently shaped things in their own bag or pillowcase. These could be things like a spoon, a comb, a hat, a small teddy bear, a pencil, a ring, a rubber band, a toy block, or anything!

When you have both collected all your things, come back together. Now name one of the things in your bag and ask your friend to reach in without looking and find that thing. If your friend pulls out the right thing, it stays out. If not, they have to put it back in the bag. The first person to empty the other person's bag is the winner!

# Helping Children Get the Most out of the SHAPES Volume

The activities on the previous page will help your child expand his or her knowledge, skills, and self-confidence. Young children learn best when they use all their senses. They need to touch, explore, experiment. Most importantly, the experience should be fun!

**Where Is My Shape?** Adults and children can have fun playing this game together and your participation can help a child sharpen his or her visual skills. When they are looking for an object you've chosen, they may get a chance to identify shapes they might not have noticed without your hints - a triangular dish, a globe, etc.

**Shapes Treasure Hunt.** Depending on their age, children might need a bit of guidance for this game. Make sure there are plenty of objects within the children's sight and reach. Put a stamp, a rubber band, a rectangular sponge where they can find them, for example. In any room, give the children a chance to find their chosen shapes on their own. Older children won't need much guidance for hunting, but if you are directing the activity and they miss an object, gently turn their attention to its location with subtle hints, such as 'Do you see something square on the window sill?' The children will get greater enjoyment and satisfaction from the game, and will begin to quickly recognize particular shapes, if they can find the shapes themselves without being told exactly where they are. Give occasional hints to any child who wants or needs one, but don't be too eager to help a child who likes to be more challenged. At the end of the game, praise all the children for their efforts, not just the 'winner.'

**Shapes in the Bag.** Give each child a container that's not see-through, such as a bag or pillowcase. If more than two children are playing, or you're playing with them, each player should search the bag belonging to the person on their left (or right) so that the game moves along in a circular motion and everyone gets a turn. If you are directing the activity, help the children find small objects to put in their bags. The best choices are objects that are familiar to them and easy to name, so that they feel a sense of accomplishment when they identify something by feeling it rather than seeing it.

Illustrations by Joseph Taylor.

© 2005 by Encyclopædia Britannica, Inc.

Second Printing, 2006

International Standard Book Number: 1-59339-103-X

Britannica Discovery Library:
Volume 7: Shapes 2005

Britannica.com may be accessed on the Internet at http://www.britannica.com.